Y

THE LIFE CYCLE OF A

SNAIL

By L.L. Owens

Published by The Child's World®
1980 Lookout Drive
Mankato, MN 56003-1705
800-599-READ
www.childsworld.com

The Child's World®: Mary Berendes, Publishing Director
The Design Lab: Kathleen Petelinsek, design
Red Line Editorial: Editorial direction

Photographs ©: Bigstock, cover (top left, bottom right), 1 (top left, bottom right), 14, 31 (bottom); Shutterstock Images, cover (top right, bottom left), 1 (top right, bottom left), 6; Amy Johansson/ Shutterstock Images, 3, 17; Sergey Toronto/Shutterstock Images, 5; Travel Bug/Shutterstock Images, 9; Juris Sturainis/ Shutterstock Images, 10, 31 (top); Bayu Harsa/Bigstock, 13, 30; Rusty Dodson/Shutterstock Images, 18; Melanie Kintz/ Shutterstock Images, 21; Malcolm Schuyl/FLPA/Photolibrary, 22; Tomas Skopa/Shutterstock Images, 25; B Borrell Casals/ FLPA/Photolibrary, 26; Eliane Haykal/iStockphoto, 29

ISBN: 978-1-60973-191-5
LCCN: 2011927741

Printed in the United States of America
Mankato, MN
July 2011
PA02089

TABLE OF

CONTENTS

Life Cycles...4

Snails...7

Laying Eggs...12

Hatchlings...15

Growing...16

In the Food Chain...19

Making New Snails...24

The Life Cycle Goes On...28

Life Cycle Diagram...30

Web Sites and Books...32

Glossary...32

Index...32

LIFE CYCLES

Every living thing has a life cycle. A life cycle is the steps a living thing goes through as it grows and changes. Humans have a life cycle. Animals have a life cycle. Plants have a life cycle, too.

A cycle is something that happens over and over again. A life cycle begins with the start of a new life. It continues as a plant or creature grows. And it keeps going as one living thing creates another, or **reproduces**—and the cycle starts over again.

A snail's life cycle has three main steps: egg, hatchling, and adult snail.

Snails **hatch** from eggs, grow, and become adults that reproduce.

Water snails live in either freshwater or saltwater.

SNAILS

Common garden snails are often found in backyards or parks. Scientists have discovered more than 40,000 species of snails around the world. The smallest are the size of a pinhead, and the largest grow to be about 30 inches (76 cm). Some snails live on land, but most snails live in water. Snails need plenty of moisture to survive, but they can be found in many different places—even the desert.

Snails are part of a group of animals called **gastropods** that have moist, soft bodies. Slugs are also part of this group. But snails are different because they have hard shells on their backs. The shell is their home. A snail can pull its whole body inside its shell. Shells come in many shapes and colors.

Snails have a big, muscular foot they use to move around. The foot ripples to move the snail forward. It is covered in slime, which helps slide the snail along its path. Snails glide along surfaces. They move across wooded trails or up tree branches. Snails living in rivers and oceans do not swim. Just like land snails, they travel by gliding on their foot.

Snail shells can be smooth and rounded or pointed and covered in spikes. The shell of a murex snail is spiky.

Snails can tell the difference between light and dark, but they do not see other things very well.

Snails have two pairs of horns, or **tentacles**, on their heads. The short ones help snails feel out their surroundings—like fingers. They also help the snails smell and sense sound vibrations. Snails' eyes are at the tips of the longer tentacles.

Inside their mouths, snails have an eating tool called a **radula**. Long like a ribbon, the radula is covered with thousands of tiny teeth-like spikes. Snails eat by pressing their radula against a plant or other food and scraping off bits to swallow. Snails scrape so hard they make holes in garden lettuce leaves.

SNAIL

LAYING EGGS

A snail's life cycle begins inside an egg.
Snail eggs can come in many different colors,
depending on the type of snail. Land snails
often lay their eggs in several clusters of
20 to 30 eggs. You might find snail egg
clusters under a flowerpot, a shrub, or any
other damp, protected spot in the soil.

Apple snails are freshwater snails. They lay pink eggs.

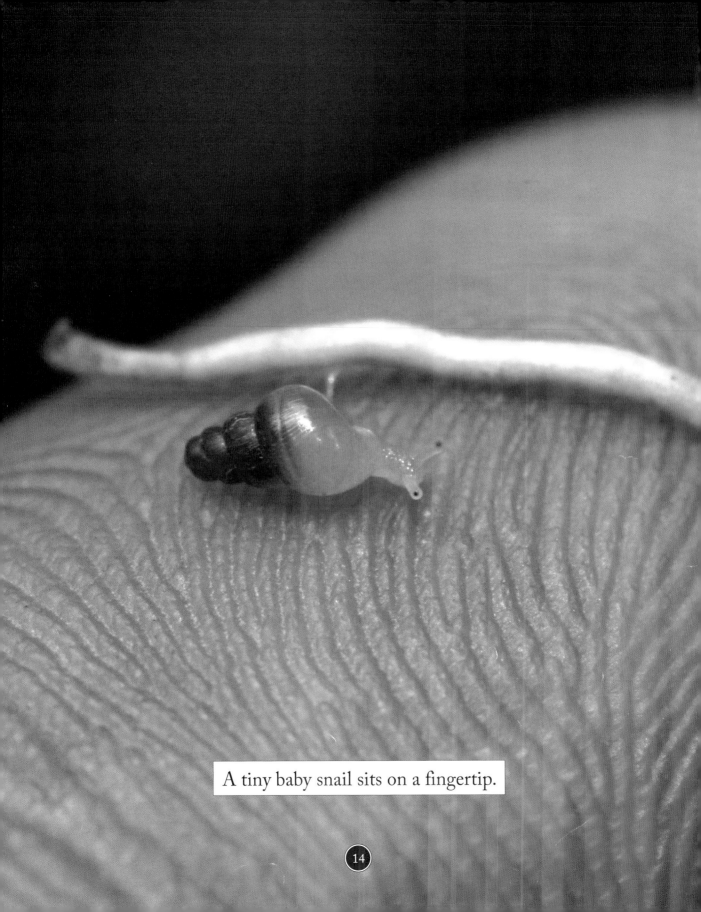

A tiny baby snail sits on a fingertip.

HATCHLINGS

A just-hatched snail is called a hatchling. It is about the same shape as an adult. But it is tiny, and its shell is very soft. The first thing a hatchling does is look for food. It might start by eating its own eggshell and unhatched eggs.

Many snails hide during the day and look for food at night. In the dark, their tentacles feel and smell for their favorite foods. Many snails eat just plants. Others, like wolf snails, eat meat—including other snails. Baby snails must look out for **predators**. Even small animals, such as toads, can gobble a tiny hatchling.

GROWING

As a snail's body grows, its shell grows with it. The oldest part of the shell is in the center of the spiral. The snail was born with that part. The outer edges of the shell are the newer parts.

Snail shells come in many shapes, sizes, and colors.
The shell of a forest snail is often brown.

Willets and other shorebirds hunt for snails on beaches.

IN THE FOOD CHAIN

The snail is an important part of the food chain. It is food for some birds and other animals, such as turtles. One species of bird eats so many snails that it's called the "snail kite."

Some predators have learned how to break into snail shells. Birds can poke their sharp bills into the shell's opening and dig out the juicy flesh.

From the moment it hatches, a snail knows how to use its senses to stay alive. It must stay safe from predators. If a snail feels a vibration with its tentacles, it knows danger is near. It can crawl away and hide or pull itself into its shell.

A snail can pull its body into its shell to hide from predators.

Snails **hibernate** together in a space in a wall.

Snails also need to protect themselves from harsh weather. Land snails hibernate to get through the cold winter. In the fall, they find a safe place under a rock or a pile of leaves. They snuggle deep into their shells. Slime covers the opening of each shell to trap in warmth. They will sleep until springtime. They live off body fat until the first warm rain of spring. Then they wake up hungry!

Snails can also survive in hot weather. In some deserts, there are long periods with no rain. When this happens, snails can seal into their shells until the rain comes. They can live like this for years without eating or moving.

MAKING NEW SNAILS

Many snails reach adulthood and are able to reproduce, or create baby snails, by age two. In many snail species, each snail has both male and female parts. Some snails reproduce alone. These snails can **fertilize** their own eggs.

Other snails reproduce in pairs. During mating, a pair of land snails covers each other in slime. They press their feet together. Sperm from each snail passes into the other. The fertilized eggs begin to grow in each snail's body. The pair separates and each snail goes its own way.

Different snail species reproduce in different ways.

A hole in the soil is a good place for a land snail to lay eggs.

26

A few weeks after mating, the snail looks for a safe place to lay its eggs. It might choose a small, moist hole in the ground or under a large, shady plant.

Depending on the species, a snail may lay about 100 eggs. Inside the eggs, tiny snail babies, called **embryos**, grow. Only some of those eggs survive. Predators might eat them. The rain washes others away. Sometimes humans step on them or dig them up without ever knowing.

S N A I L

THE LIFE CYCLE GOES ON

The eggs hatch two to four weeks later. New baby snails are born. And the life cycle continues. How long a snail lives depends on its kind. A garden snail might live between one and five years. Some freshwater snails live 15 years. Other types of snails may live 20 or 30 years.

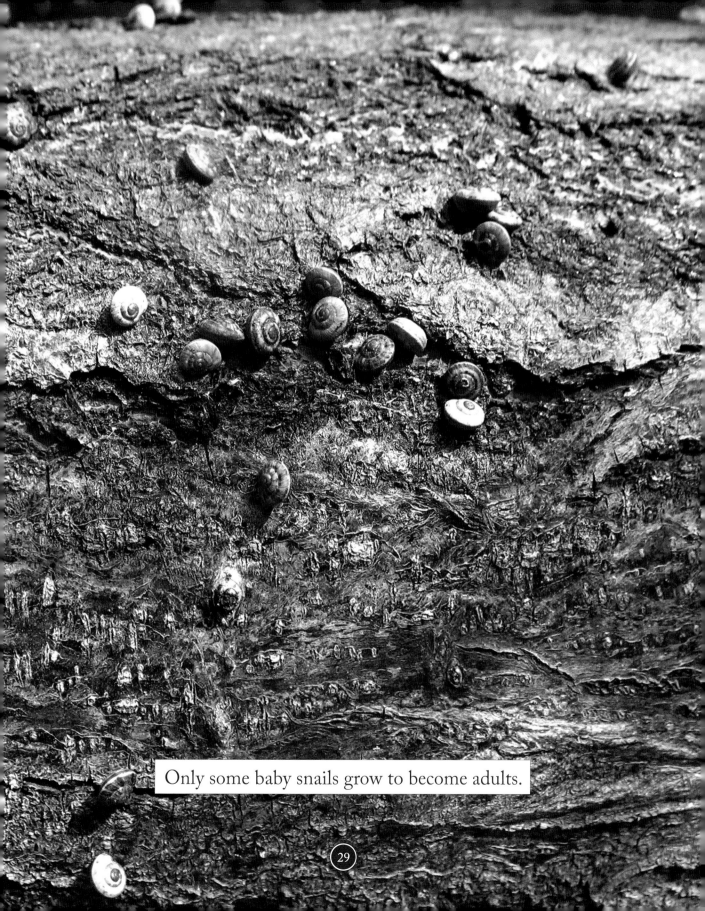

Only some baby snails grow to become adults.

LIFE CYCLE DIAGRAM

Egg

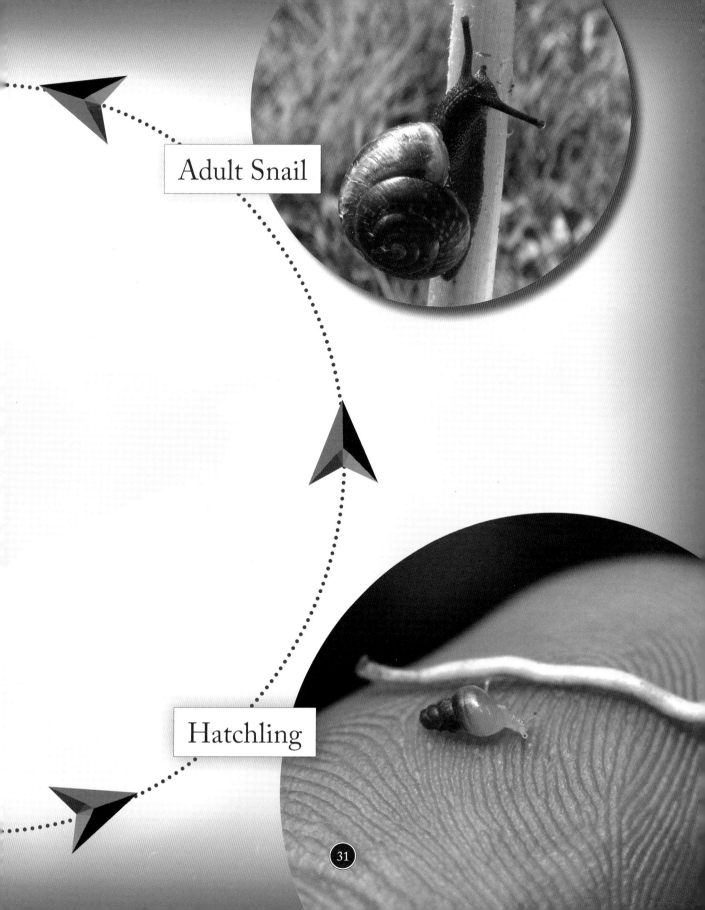

Adult Snail

Hatchling

Web Sites

Visit our Web site for links about the life cycle of a snail:
childsworld.com/links

Note to Parents, Teachers, and Librarians: We routinely verify our Web links to make sure they are safe and active sites. So encourage your readers to check them out!

Books

Amato, Carol. *Backyard Pets: Activities for Exploring Wildlife Close to Home.* New York, NY: Wiley, 2002.

Campbell, Sarah C. *Wolfsnail: A Backyard Predator.* Honesdale, PA: Boyds Mills Press, 2008.

Woodward, John. *Snail.* New York, NY: Chelsea House, 2010.

Glossary

embryos (EM-bree-ohs): Embryos are organisms in the early stages of growth. Snail embryos grow inside eggs.

fertilize (FUR-tuh-lize): To fertilize is when a male reproductive cell joins a female reproductive cell to create a new life. Some snails have both male and female parts and can fertilize their own eggs.

gastropods (GASS-truh-pawdz): Gastropods are a type of soft-bodied animal with a head, a muscular foot that moves them forward, and often a coiled shell. Snails are gastropods.

hatch (HACH): To hatch is to break out of an egg. After baby snails hatch, they are called hatchlings.

hibernate (HYE-bur-nate): To hibernate, an animal or insect spends the winter in a deep sleep, with slowed breathing and heartbeat. Sometimes, large groups of land snails hibernate together.

predators (PRED-uh-turs): Predators are animals that hunt and eat other animals. Snail predators include turtles and some birds.

radula (RA-juh-luh): A radula is an eating tool in a snail's mouth covered with thousands of tooth-like bumps. A snail uses its radula to tear through food.

reproduces (ree-pruh-DOOS-ez): If an animal or plant reproduces, it produces offspring. A snail reproduces and makes baby snails.

tentacles (TEN-tuh-kullz): Tentacles are long feelers or limbs that come out from the bodies of some animals. Snails have two sets of tentacles—one set is for feeling and one set has eyes.

Index

birds, 19

desert, 7, 23

egg, 4, 12, 15, 24, 27–28
embryos, 27
eyes, 11

food, 11, 15, 19
food chain, 19
foot, 8

garden snails, 7, 28
gastropods, 8
growth, 4, 7, 16, 24, 27

hatching, 15, 20, 28
hatchling, 4, 15
hibernating, 23
hiding, 15, 20

laying eggs, 12, 27
life span, 28

predators, 15, 19–20, 27

radula, 11
reproduction, 4, 24

shells, 8, 15, 16, 19, 20, 23, 27
size, 7
slime, 8, 23, 24
slugs, 8
"snail kite," 19

tentacles, 11, 15, 20
toads, 15
turtles, 19

wolf snail, 15